Mathstraks:
Algebra

Creative tasks, activities
and games for ages 11-14

Lesley Higgin

tarquin

The Mathstraks Series

Mathstraks Algebra is part of a a series of books, published by Tarquin. More details, and full contents, are available on the website.

Mathstraks Geometry

Sheets in this *Mathstraks: Geometry* volume include:
• Angle tangle
• Properties of quadrilaterals
• Polygon properties
• Quad squad
• Bearing codes
• Measure for treasure
• Area puzzles
• Cubes and cuboids
• Prism patterns
• Co-ordinates and reflections
• Transformations

Mathstraks Number

Sheets in this *Mathstraks: Number* volume include:
• Negative multiplication walls
• Equivalent fractions
• Fraction boxes
• Percentages
• Decimal sequences
• Function chains
• If...then
• Four Special Numbers
• Phone a friend and other practical problems
• Indices

Distributed in the USA by Parkwest
www.parkwestpubs.com
www.amazon.com & major retailers

Distributed in Australia by OLM
www.lat-olm.com.au

© 2011: Lesley Higgin   www.tarquingroup.com
ISBN: 978 1 907550 13 3
Printed and designed in the UK   All rights reserved

tarquin publications
Suite 74, 17 Holywell Hill
St Albans, AL1 1DT, UK

Welcome to Mathstraks: Algebra

Algebra is a fascinating and vital part of the mathematics curriculum, but all too often text books deal with it in a dry and prescriptive way, removing all the fun and interest along the way.

I have developed the Mathstraks materials to enable pupils to gain a solid understanding of the subject through fun, challenge and play. Examples of the use of algebra to solve real-life problems have been included to improve functional skills. I have used the materials for many years in my own classroom and have found them to be very effective and enjoyable for pupils and teacher alike!

The activities are aimed at ages 11-14, but can also be used as extension material for some primary school children and as revision or starter activities for older pupils.

I hope you find the book useful and, most importantly, that the children enjoy it.

Lesley Higgin

Mathstraks: Algebra

Creative tasks, activities and games for ages 11-14
Lesley Higgin

Family Photos

Use the clues to work out expressions for the ages of Billy's relatives.

Billy's little sister
is 6 years younger
than Billy

Gran is 3 years
younger than
Grandad

Dad was 25 when
Billy was born

Billy is x years
old

Grandad is 8
times as old
as Billy

Mum is 1 year
older than Dad

Name the Teacher

The ages of each teacher are written algebraically under each picture.
Use these clues to work out the name of each teacher!

- Mrs Bunsen is 5 years older than Miss Mathews.
- Mr White is 4 years younger than Mrs Bunsen.
- Mrs Priestley and Mr Maplin are the same age.
- Miss Mathews is twice as old as Frau Weiss.
- Miss Bite is as old as Mr White and Mrs Bunsen together.
- Mrs Old is a year younger than Mr Maplin.
- Miss Philips-Edwards is 3 times as old as Miss Mathews.
- Miss Cook is 8 years younger than Mr White.
- Senor Blanco is the same age as Miss Bite and Mr White together.
- Mrs Bunsen is a year older than Mademoiselle Blanche.

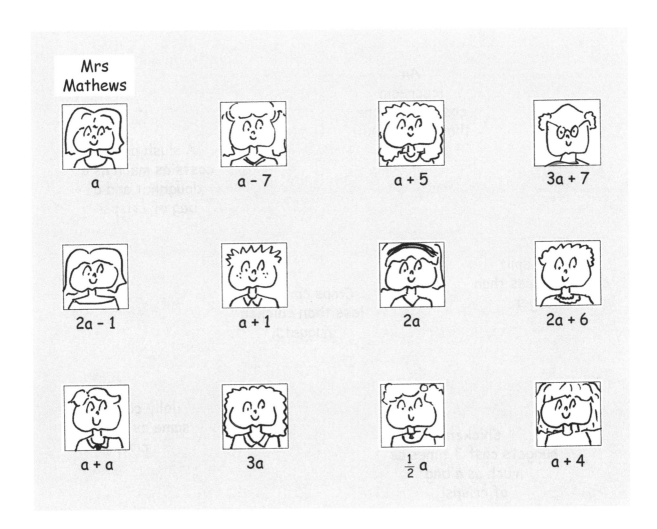

Cathy's Café

Use the customer comments to work out expressions for the cost of each item in the café.

Start with the cost of a bag of crisps as c pence.

Customer Comments

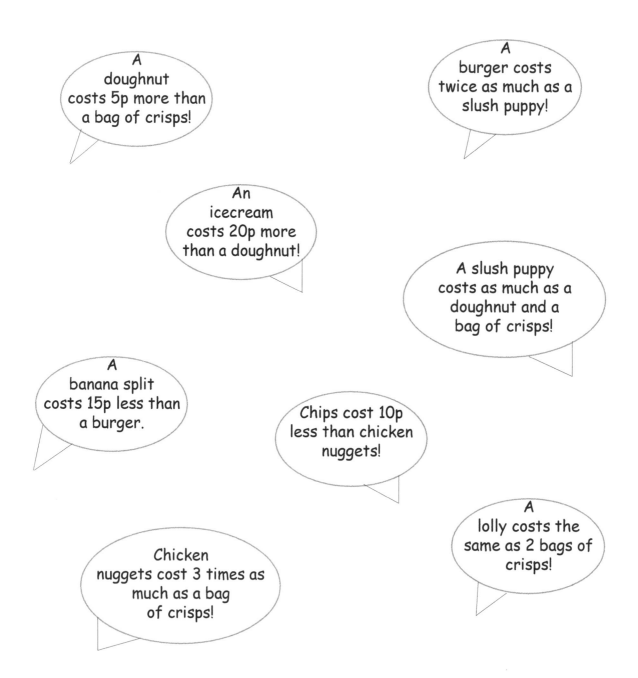

A doughnut costs 5p more than a bag of crisps!

A burger costs twice as much as a slush puppy!

An icecream costs 20p more than a doughnut!

A slush puppy costs as much as a doughnut and a bag of crisps!

A banana split costs 15p less than a burger.

Chips cost 10p less than chicken nuggets!

A lolly costs the same as 2 bags of crisps!

Chicken nuggets cost 3 times as much as a bag of crisps!

Lunch at Kev's Café

Menu

Item	Price in p
Chips	w
Cola	w − 10
Milkshake	w + 5
Burger	2w
Pizza	2w + 5
Icecream	3w − 10
Sandwich	2w − 20

1. Work out expression for the total price of these lunch orders.
   (Write your answers as simply as possible)

Order 1

2 chips

1 milkshake

1 burger

Order 2

3 milkshakes

1 pizza

1 sandwich

Order 3

2 pizzas

1 colas

1 ice cream

2. The lunch order for table 6 came to a total of 8w + 20.
   What do you think they ordered?

3. The lunch order for table 2 came to 10w − 5.
   What do you think they ordered?

Algebra Dominoes

Cut out the algebra dominoes cards.

Match them so that each card is next to a card with an equivalent expression.

For example:

$$2x^2 + x \quad | \quad 2(x + 1) \qquad \longleftrightarrow \qquad 2x + 2 \quad | \quad \dfrac{4x - 2}{2}$$

The set of cards can be arranged to form a closed loop.

- Try this for yourself

- Record how you matched the dominoes in your loop.

Algebra Dominoes Cards

$\dfrac{4x + 2}{2}$	$x(2 - x)$

$2(2x - 1)$	$2x + 1$

$2x - 1$	$x(x + 2)$

$2x - x^2$	$2x - 2$

$2(2 - x)$	$x(2x + 1)$

$2x + 2$	$\dfrac{4x - 2}{2}$

$2(x - 1)$	$x^2 - 2x$

$4x + 4$	$4 - 2x$

$x + 2$	$4(x + 1)$

$x^2 + 2x$	$4x - 2$

$2x^2 + x$	$2(x + 1)$

$x(x - 2)$	$\dfrac{2x + 4}{2}$

Expressions

In each of the following expressions, n is a positive integer.

$2n$	$4n$	$2n^2$
$(2n)^2$	$3n^2$	$4n^2$
$n+2$	$2n+3$	$2(n+3)$
$3n+1$	$3(n+1)$	$6n-3$
$3(2n+1)$	$4n+1$	$12n$

Which of these expressions will **always** be:

1. odd

2. even

3. a multiple of 3

4. a multiple of 4

5. square

Algebra Chains

A. Use two of the following operations to complete the algebra chains:

| + a | x a | + 1 | x 2 |

1. 6 → [ ] → [ ] → $12+2a$

2. a → [ ] → [ ] → $2a+1$

3. 3b → [ ] → [ ] → $6b+2$

4. 2a → [ ] → [ ] → $5a$

5. a+b → [ ] → [ ] → $4a+2b$

6. b → [ ] → [ ] → $ab+a^2$

7. b-a → [ ] → [ ] → $2b-a$

8. 5a → [ ] → [ ] → $10a^2$

9. 4 → [ ] → [ ] → $5a$

10. $\frac{1}{2}a$ → [ ] → [ ] → $a+2$

B. Use 3 operations to produce a chain to get from:

1. a to $4a+1$

2. 2b to $2ab + 2a$

3. 3 to $6a^2$

Algebra Tricks

- Try both of the following function machines with 3 different numbers.

- What do you think is happening?

- Prove your theory using algebra.

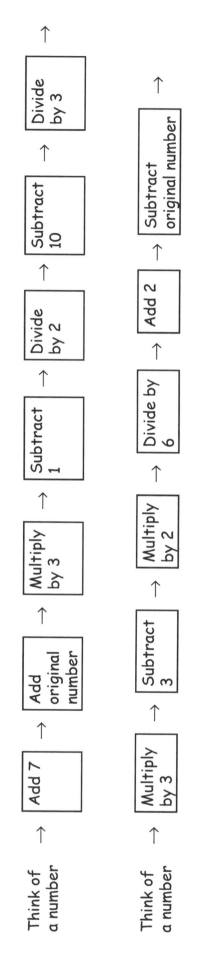

Think of a number → Add 7 → Add original number → Multiply by 3 → Subtract 1 → Divide by 2 → Subtract 10 → Divide by 3 →

Think of a number → Multiply by 3 → Subtract 3 → Multiply by 2 → Divide by 6 → Add 2 → Subtract original number →

- Now make up a function machine of your own.

- Say what is meant to happen and prove it using algebra

Function Machines

input $\rightarrow$ | ? | $\rightarrow$ output

If x is the input, write down the output for the following function machines:

1. add 4

2. multiply by 3

3. add 4 then multiply by 3

4. multiply by 3 then add 4

5. divide by 2

6. divide by 2 then add 7

7. add 7 then divide by 2

8. square

9. square then subtract 2

10. subtract 2 then square

11. subtract from 10

12. multiply by 5 then subtract 7 then square

More Function Machines

Describe what the following number machines are doing:

1. x $\rightarrow$? $\rightarrow$ $5x$

2. x $\rightarrow$? $\rightarrow$ $2x - 6$

3. x $\rightarrow$? $\rightarrow$ $5(x + 1)$

4. x $\rightarrow$? $\rightarrow$ $x^2 + 1$

5. x $\rightarrow$? $\rightarrow$ $2x^2$

6. x $\rightarrow$? $\rightarrow$ $(2x)^2$

7. x $\rightarrow$? $\rightarrow$ $6 - x$

8. x $\rightarrow$? $\rightarrow$ $\dfrac{x + 3}{4}$

9. x $\rightarrow$? $\rightarrow$ $3x^2 - 4$

10. x $\rightarrow$? $\rightarrow$ $3(x^2 - 4)$

11. x $\rightarrow$? $\rightarrow$ $3(x - 4)^2$

12. x $\rightarrow$? $\rightarrow$ $(x^2 + 4)^2$

Function Fix

x2	x2	x3	x3	x5

square	+2	+1	+6	-1

- The function listed above can be arranged to form function machines.

- Use the clues below to fill in the gaps in the function machines.
  (Assume that the input number is a positive integer)

The output for machine A is always odd.

B and C give the same output, which is always a multiple of 3.

If machine D has an input of 10, then the output is 99.

The output for machine E is always a multiple of 10.

A. input → ☐ → ☐ → output

B. input → ☐ → ☐ → output

C. input → ☐ → ☐ → output

D. input → ☐ → ☐ → output

E. input → ☐ → ☐ → output

Now write all your function machines algebraically using 'n' as your input number.

Dice Sequences

Throw two dice and write down the values, smallest first, in the boxes below. (If both scores are the same, throw again)

If these two values are the first two terms of an arithmetic sequence, fill in the next three values in the spaces above.

What is the nth term of your sequence?

Now throw the dice again and repeat the above until you have 7 different sequences. Fill your results in the spaces below:

dice scores	rest of sequence	n^{th} term

How many different sequences is it possible to make in this way?

Algebra Line of Four

- This is a game for 2-3 players.

- Throw a six-sided dice. Then choose an expression from the 'algebra box' and substitute the value on the dice into the expression.

- Find this number on the playing grid and colour it in your colour.

- Now your partner throws the dice, substitutes and colours a number in their colour.

- If your number has already been coloured then you miss a go.

- The winner is the first player to get a line of four.

Algebra Box

$4n-1$	n^2	$2n^2$
$20-2n$	n^2-2	$40-n^2$

Playing Grid

7	50	36	9	12	72
18	8	4	34	16	2
1	16	3	7	14	23
11	23	18	32	36	8
12	15	19	4	24	25
31	2	14	39	10	15

Substitution Bingo

This is a good end of lesson activity.

Pupils should draw out a 4×4 grid in their books.

In this grid they write the numbers from 1 to 20 inclusive (no repeats). Then write on the board: a = 2, b = 4, c = 3

Call out numbers algebraically in a random order:

1. b - c
2. b - a
3. a + b - c
4. a^2
5. a + c
6. 2b - a
7. a + 2b - c
8. ab
9. c^2
10. 2a + 2c
11. 2b + c
12. bc
13. 2b + a + c
14. ab + ac
15. c^2 + a + b
16. b^2
17. 4b + c - a
18. 2a + 2b + 2c
19. a + 2b + 3c
20. $a^2 + b^2$

Pupils cross off numbers on their grid.

They should first aim to get a line, then a full house.

Values of a, b and c can be changed and you can make harder or easier expressions for each number.

Substitution 1

If a = 2, b = 1, c = 4, d = 3 and f = 6 work out the value of the expression in each box and shade them in as follows:

2 – red, 4 – yellow, 5 – green, 10 – blue

f+c	c+2d	a+b	f+b	c+2b	c+d	3c-d	2f-d	f+a	3b+f	2d-b	3d-c
2d	2c+a	2f-c	3d	2c	b+c+d	f+d	ad	2c-a	2a+b	c-a+b
3a+c	2f-a	c-b	d+b	c+a	3d-a	d-b	a+b+c	ac	a+d	2c-d
2d+b	3d+b	2d-a	4a	2c-b	2b	c-a	f-c	a+b+d	b+c	d+f-b
b+d+f	3c-a	f-a	f-2b	2c+b	f-c+b	2c-3a	f+2b	c+d+a	f-b	3a+d

Now work out the answer!

Substitution 2

If $a = 2$, $b = 1$, $c = 4$, $d = 3$ and $f = 6$, work out the value of the expression in each box and shade them in as follows:

2 – red, 4 – yellow, 5 – green, 10 – blue

d^2+b	$ad+c$	d^2-b	db	$(f-d)^2$	$ad+b$	$a+c$	$a+c$	$2f-d$	bf	d^2-a^2	$ad-b$
$a-b^2$	$a(b+c)$	$a+f$	$5a-b$	$d+c$	$abd-d$	$d-a$	bd	$\frac{1}{2}c^2$	fb	a^2+b	d^2-a
$cd-a$	c^2-f	$cd-f$	a^2	$f-a$	$db+c$	$d(d-a)$	$2c-f$	$ac+b$	a^2+b+c	$2a^2-d$	$f-b$
d^2	$2f-a$	$\frac{1}{2}a$	$d+b$	d^2-ad	ac	$\frac{1}{2}c$	$f-c$	$2a^2-f$	$af-c$	$ac-d$	ca
$2(f-b)$	$5a$	$3d$	$c(d-a)$	bc	$2a^2$	$2c+b$	$fd-c^2$	d^2-d	$d-a$	d^2-c	$d(f-c)$

Now work out the answer!

Algebra Ink Spl█dges

Jo has done her algebra homework, but it has got splattered with ink! Your task is to rewrite her homework, including working, so that it can be marked.

1. $2x + 1 = 17$
   $2x = █$
   $x = █$

2. $2x - 5 = 21$
   $2x = █$
   $x = █$

3. $3x - 2 = 10$
   $3x = █$
   $x = █$

4. $3x + 4 = 31$
   $3x = █$
   $x = █$

5. $5x + 1 = 41$
   $5x = █$
   $x = █$

6. $3 + 2x = 16$
   $2x = █$
   $x = █$

7. $2x + █ = 7$
   $2x = 4$
   $x = █$

8. $5x - █ = 16$
   $5x = █$
   $x = 4$

9. $10x + 2 = 21$
   $10x = █$
   $x = █$

10. $4x + 12 = 22$
   $4x = █$
   $x = █$

Ages

1. Andy, Brenda and Cath give the following clues about their ages:

'Brenda is 14 years older than Andy'

'Cath and Brenda are the same age'

'Cath is 3 times as old as Andy'

Taking Andy's age to be 'n':

a) Write down an expression for Brenda's age.

b) Write down a different expression for Cath's age.

c) Form an equation in n and solve your equation to find Andy's age.

d) Work out the ages of Brenda and Cathy.

2. Ed, Fran and Dave give these clues about their ages:

'Fran is 13 years younger than Ed'

'Ed is twice as old as Dave'

'Fran is 5 years older than Dave'

Taking Dave's age to be 'x':

a) Write down an expression for Ed's age.

b) Write down 2 expressions for Fran's age.

c) Form an equation in x and solve your equation to find Dave's age.

d) Work out the ages of Ed and Fran.

Hiring a Car

The following car hire companies all have different ways of working out the cost (in pounds).

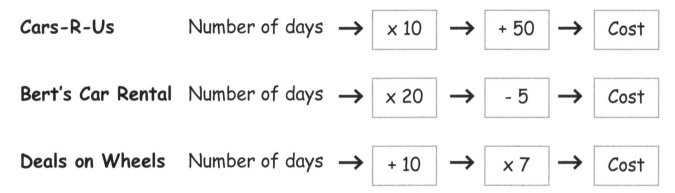

1. How much would it cost to hire a car from each company for one day?

2. How much would it cost to hire a car from each company for 2 days?

3. Work out expressions for the cost to hire a car from each company for n days.

4. Tim hired a car from Cars-R-Us. It cost him £120. For how many days did he hire the car? Did he get the best deal?

5. Rachel hired a car from Bert's Car Rental. It cost her £75. For how many days did she hire the car? Did she get the best deal?

6. Sue hired a car from Deals on Wheels. It cost her £140. For how many days did she hire the car. Did she get the best deal?

7. Another car hire company makes the following charges:

No of days	Cost
1	85
2	90
3	95
4	100
5	105

What rule is the company using to work out these charges?

Polygon Plot

- Draw each set of lines on new −8 to 8 axes
- When you have drawn all the lines you should see a polygon in the middle of the axes.
- Shade in the polygon and write down its name.

Polygon 1: $y = 4x + 6$
$y = -4x + 6$
$y = -2$

Polygon 2: $y = 2x + 6$
$y = 2x - 6$
$y = -2x + 6$
$y = -2x - 6$

Polygon 3: $y = 2$
$y = -1$
$y = 3x - 7$
$y = 3x + 8$

Polygon 4: $y = 6x - 8$
$y = -6x - 8$
$y = x + 6$
$y = -x + 6$

Points and Lines

- This is a game for 2 players.

- Each pair needs a pair of axes from 0 to 8 axes and a set of line cards.

- Each player should use a different coloured pen.

- Shuffle the line cards and place them in the centre.

- Take a line card and plot one point that would be on that line.

- For example, if you picked the line card $y = 2x$ then one of the points you could plot is (3, 6)

- Now your partner picks a card and plots their chosen point.

  The winner is the first player to get a line of 4 points plotted. (horizontal, vertical or diagonal).

Points and Lines - line cards

$y = x$	$y = x + 1$	$y = x + 4$
$y = x + 6$	$y = x - 2$	$y = x - 5$
$y = x - 3$	$y = x + 3$	$y = x - 7$
$y = x - 4$	$y = x + 5$	$y = 10 - x$
$y = 8 - x$	$y = 6 - x$	$y = x/2$
$y = 2x$	$y = 2x + 3$	$y = 3x$
$y = 3x + 5$	$y = 2x - 4$	$y = x - 1$
$x = 6$	$x = 8$	$x = 7$
$y = 0$	$y = 5$	$y = 1$

Teacher's Notes and Answers

Family Photos

Notes
This is a good introductory activity to algebraic expressions.
The idea of connections between family's ages can first be dealt with using a numerical example, then generalised.

Pupils usually cope with the notation 2 x x = $2x$ quite naturally.

A useful extension activity is to draw a new member of the family on the board along with an expression for their age.

Eg. 'Uncle Herbert's age is $4x + 1$'

Pupils have to describe Uncle Herbert's age in as many ways as they can.

Answers
Little sister: $x - 6$ Dad: $x + 25$ Mum: $x + 26$

Grandad: $8x$ Gran: $8x - 3$

Name the Teacher

Notes
This activity should follow on from some introductory work on algebraic expressions ('Family Photos' could be used)

The activity encourages pupils to think about what algebraic expressions mean and also introduces use of standard notation such as 2 x a = 2a and simplifying expressions such as a + 1 + a + 5 = 2a + 6.

As an extension activity, the following could be drawn on the board:

3 a + 5

Pupils could then be asked to find different ways of describing Mr Heads' age. Eg: 'Mr Head is the same age as Mrs Priestley and Mrs Bunsen together'. This could then lead onto some useful class discussion and further work on simplification of algebraic expressions.

Answers

Expression	Teacher	Expression	Teacher
a	Miss Mathews	2a	Mrs Priestley
a - 7	Miss Cook	2a + 6	Miss Bite
a + 5	Mrs Bunsen	a + a	Mr Maplin
3a + 7	Senor Blanco	3a	Miss P-E
2a - 1	Mrs Old	$\frac{1}{2}$a	Frau Weiss
a + 1	Mr White	a + 4	Mme Blanche

Cathy's Café

Notes

As an extension activity, an order could be written on the board and the pupils have to write down, as simply as possible, an expression for the total cost.

Eg:

    2 doughnuts
    1 slush puppy
    2 chips
    1 icecream

    Total   _____

Answers

Item	Expression in pence
Crisps	c
Doughnut	$c + 5$
Slush Puppy	$2c + 5$
Chicken Nuggets	$3c$
Chips	$3c - 10$
Burger	$4c + 10$
Ice Cream	$c + 25$
Lolly	$2c$
Banana Split	$4c - 5$

Lunch at Kev's Café

Notes

This activity practises collecting like terms.

It also indirectly introduces multiplying out brackets.

For example, the cost of 2 pizzas is calculated by doing $2(2w + 5)$.

Answers

1.   Order 1
2 chips	$2w$
1 milkshake	$w + 5$
1 burger	$2w$
Total	$5w + 5$

      Order 2
3 milkshakes	$3w + 15$
1 pizza	$2w + 5$
1 sandwich	$2w - 20$
Total	$7w$

      Order 3
2 pizzas	$4w + 10$
1 cola	$w - 10$
1 icecream	$3w - 10$
Total	$8w - 10$

2.   Many possible answers
   eg. 4 pizzas or 4 milkshakes + 1 burger + 2 chips

3.   Many possible answers
   eg. 1 icecream + 6 chips + 1 milkshake or 3 pizzas + 1 sandwich + 1 burger

Expressions

Notes

It must be stressed to pupils that there are some expressions which can take all sorts of different values. For example, 'n+2', could be odd or even. However, the expression '2n' can only ever be even.

Answers

1. Odd: $2n+3$, $4n+1$, $3(2n+1)$

2. Even: $2n$, $4n$, $2n^2$, $(2n)^2$, $4n^2$, $2(n+3)$, $12n$

3. Multiple of 3: $3n^2$, $3(n+1)$, $6n - 3$, $3(2n+1)$, $12n$

4. Multiple of 4: $4n$, $(2n)^2$, $4n^2$, $12n$

5. Square: $(2n)^2$, $4n^2$ (these expressions are equivalent)

Algebra Chains

A. Answers

1.   6   → | + a | → | × 2 | → | 12+2a |

2.   a   → | × 2 | → | + 1 | → | 2a+1 |

3.   3b   → | + 1 | → | × 2 | → | 6b+2 |

4.   2a   → | × 2 | → | + a | → | 5a |

5.   a+b   → | + a | → | × 2 | → | 4a+2b |

6.   b   → | +a | → | × a | → | $ab+a^2$ |

7.   b-a   → | × 2 | → | + a | → | 2b-a |

8.   5a   → | × 2 | → | × a | → | $10a^2$ |

9.   4   → | × a | → | + a | → | 5a |

10. $\frac{1}{2}$a   → | + 1 | → | × 2 | → | a+2 |

(The operations in question 8 could also be the other way round)

B.   Answers (there may be other answers)

1.   a → | + a | → | × 2 | → | + 1 | → 4a + 1

2.   2b → | + 1 | → | × a | → | + a | → 2ab + 2a

3.   3 → | × a | → | × 2 | → | × a | → $6a^2$

Algebra Tricks

Notes

This activity requires some previous discussion/practice on using algebra to represent 'any number'. A similar example could be used as a starter activity to begin the lesson.

Answers

The first function machine has its output as the original number.

This can be proved by using ' x ' as the original number:

$$x \rightarrow x+7 \rightarrow 2x+7 \rightarrow 6x+21 \rightarrow 6x+20 \rightarrow 3x+10 \rightarrow 3x \rightarrow x$$

The second function machine always has output 1.

This can be proved in a similar way:

$$x \rightarrow 3x \rightarrow 3x-3 \rightarrow 6x-6 \rightarrow x-1 \rightarrow x+1 \rightarrow 1$$

Function Machines

Notes

This activity practises algebraic notation and order of operations. Special attention should be drawn to questions 3 and 4 , 6 and 7 and 9 and 10, which demonstrate that the order matters.

Answers

1. $x+4$

2. $3x$

3. $3(x+4)$

4. $3x+4$

5. $\dfrac{x}{2}$

6. $\dfrac{x}{2}+7$

7. $\dfrac{x+7}{2}$

8. x^2

9. x^2-2

10. $(x-2)^2$

11. $10-x$

12. $(5x-7)^2$

More Function Machines

Answers

1. Multiply by 5

2. Multiply by 2 then subtract 6

3. Add 1 and then multiply by 5

4. Square then add 1

5. Square then multiply by 2

6. Multiply by 2 then square

7. Subtract from 6

8. Add 3 then divide by 4

9. Square then multiply by 3 then subtract 4

10. Square then subtract 4 then multiply by 3

11. Subtract 4 then square then multiply by 3

12. Square then add 4 then square

Function Fix

Answers

Written algebraically:

A. input → $\boxed{\times 2}$ → $\boxed{+ 1}$ → output $2n+1$

B. input → $\boxed{\times 3}$ → $\boxed{+ 6}$ → output $3n+6$

C. input → $\boxed{+ 2}$ → $\boxed{\times 3}$ → output $3(n+2)$

D. input → $\boxed{square}$ → $\boxed{- 1}$ → output n^2-1

E. input → $\boxed{\times 2}$ → $\boxed{\times 5}$ → output $10n$

- Machines B and C are equivalent so could be swapped.

- Machine E could also be written ×5 then ×2.

Dice Sequences

Notes

This activity combines practice at finding n^{th} terms, with logical reasoning to work out how many different sequences are possible.

The activity can be extended by considering the results for an eight-sided dice. The number of possible sequences is always a triangle number – for a d-sided dice, the number of possible sequences is $d(d-1)/2$

More able pupils could also work out the sequences and n^{th} terms obtained if the smallest number in the sequence is not written first.

Answers

All possible sequences are listed below:

Sequence					n^{th} term
1	2	3	4	5	n
1	3	5	7	9	$2n-1$
1	4	7	10	13	$3n-2$
1	5	9	13	17	$4n-3$
1	6	11	16	21	$5n-4$
2	3	4	5	6	$n+1$
2	4	6	8	10	$2n$
2	5	8	11	14	$3n-1$
2	6	10	14	18	$4n-2$
3	4	5	6	7	$n+2$
3	5	7	9	11	$2n+1$
3	6	9	12	15	$3n$
4	5	6	7	8	$n+3$
4	6	8	10	12	$2n+2$
5	6	7	8	9	$n+4$

Substitution 1 and 2

Notes

This activity provides plenty of practice in substituting numbers into algebraic expressions.

The easier (Substitution 1) and harder (Substitution 2) versions are ideal for use in a mixed ability class, as the work looks similar and has the same answer.

Answers: Substitution 1

f+c	c+2d	a+b	f+b	c+2b	c+d	3c-d	2f-d	f+a	3b+f	2d-b	3d-c
2d	2c+a	2f-c	3d	f-d	2c	b+c+d	f+d	ad	2c-a	2a+b	c-a+b
3a+c	2f-a	c-b	2a	d+b	c+a	3d-a	d-b	a+b+c	ac	a+d	2c-d
2d+b	3d+b	3d-b	2d-a	4a	2c-b	2b	c-a	f-c	a+b+d	b+c	d+f-b
b+d+f	3c-a	2d+a	f-a	f-2b	2c+b	f-c+b	2c-3a	f+2b	c+d+a	f-b	3a+d

Answers: Substitution 2

d^2+b	ad+c	d^2-b	db	$(f-d)^2$	ad+b	a+c	a+c	2f-d	bf	d^2-a^2	ad-b
$a-b^2$	a(b+c)	a+f	5a-b	d+c	abd-d	d-a	bd	$\frac{1}{2}c^2$	fb	a^2+b	d^2-a
cd-a	c^2-f	cd-f	a^2	f-a	db+c	d(d-a)	2c-f	ac+b	a^2+b+c	$2a^2-d$	f-b
d^2	2f-a	$\frac{1}{2}a$	d+b	d^2-ad	ac	$\frac{1}{2}c$	f-c	$2a^2-f$	af-c	ac-d	ca
2(f-b)	5a	3d	c(d-a)	bc	$2a^2$	2c+b	$fd-c^2$	d^2-d	d-a	d^2-c	d(f-c)

Both activities give the answer 3c + f, which, in turn, gives the answer 18.

Algebra Ink Splodges

Notes

This activity is useful to encourage pupils to set out their working clearly.

Questions 7 and 8 stretch them a stage further and should demonstrate that they understand the method.

Answers

1. $2x + 1 = 17$
    $2x = 16$
    $x = 8$

2. $2x - 5 = 21$
    $2x = 26$
    $x = 13$

3. $3x - 2 = 10$
    $3x = 12$
    $x = 4$

4. $3x + 4 = 31$
    $3x = 27$
    $x = 9$

5. $5x + 1 = 41$
    $5x = 40$
    $x = 8$

6. $3 + 2x = 16$
    $2x = 13$
    $x = 6.5$

7. $2x + 3 = 7$
    $2x = 4$
    $x = 2$

8. $5x - 4 = 16$
    $5x = 20$
    $x = 4$

9. $10x + 2 = 21$
    $10x = 19$
    $x = 1.9$

10. $4x + 12 = 22$
    $4x = 10$
    $x = 2.5$

Ages

Answers

1.

a) $n + 14$

b) $3n$

c) $3n = n + 14$ $n = 7$

d) Brenda and Cathy are both 21

2.

a) $2x$

b) $2x - 13$ and $x + 5$

c) $2x - 13 = x + 5$ $x = 18$

d) Ed is 36 and Fran is 23

Hiring a car

Answers

1

Company	Cost (£)
Cars-R-Us	60
Bert's Car Rental	15
Deals on Wheels	77

2

Company	Cost (£)
Cars-R-Us	70
Bert's Car Rental	35
Deals on Wheels	84

3

Company	Cost (£)
Cars-R-Us	10n + 50
Bert's Car Rental	20n – 5
Deals on Wheels	7(n + 10)

$$\searrow$$

Or 7n + 70.
This is a useful intro to expanding brackets

4. He hired it for 7 days. It wasn't the best deal.
It would have cost £119 with Deals on Wheels.

5. She hired it for 4 days. It was the best deal.

6. She hired it for 10 days. It was the best deal.

7. Cost = 5n + 80   (n = number of days)

Polygon Plot

Answers

Polygon 1

Isosceles triangle with vertices at: (-2,-2), (2,-2), (0,6)

Polygon 2

Rhombus with vertices at: (0,6), (0,-6), (3,0), (-3,0)

Polygon 3

Parallelogram with vertices at: (3,2), (2,-1), (-3,-1), (-2,2)

Polygon 4

Kite with vertices at: (2,4), (-2,4), (0,-8), (0,6)